STEP BY STEP PROJECTS

How to Make ICE CREAM

Tom Greve

Rourke
Educational Media

rourkeeducationalmedia.com

Scan for Related Titles
and Teacher Resources

Teaching Focus:
Consonant Blends- Look in the book to find words that begin with a consonant blend such as *dr, fl, sk*.

Before Reading:

Building Academic Vocabulary and Background Knowledge
Before reading a book, it is important to set the stage for your child or student by using pre-reading strategies. This will help them develop their vocabulary, increase their reading comprehension, and make connections across the curriculum.
1. Read the title and look at the cover. *Let's make predictions about what this book will be about.*
2. Take a picture walk by talking about the pictures/photographs in the book. Implant the vocabulary as you take the picture walk. Be sure to talk about the text features such as headings, Table of Contents, glossary, bolded words, captions, charts/diagrams, or Index.
3. Have students read the first page of text with you then have students read the remaining text.
4. Strategy Talk – use to assist students while reading.
    - Get your mouth ready
    - Look at the picture
    - Think…does it make sense
    - Think…does it look right
    - Think…does it sound right
    - Chunk it – by looking for a part you know
5. Read it again.
6. After reading the book complete the activities below.

Content Area Vocabulary

delicious
ingredients
science
supplies
toppings
transfer

After Reading:

Comprehension and Extension Activity
After reading the book, work on the following questions with your child or students in order to check their level of reading comprehension and content mastery.
1. *Why is it important to follow the directions while making ice cream?* (Summarize)
2. *What are your favorite ice cream flavors? Why?* (Text to self connection)
3. *Why is it important to shake the bag with ice and the cream mixture?* (Asking questions)
4. *What is the first thing you should do if you want to make ice cream?* (Summarize)

Extension Activity
What's the most popular ice cream flavor in your home or class? Take a survey of favorite flavors and create a tally chart. Using the tallies, create a bar graph to show the most popular flavors of ice cream.

Table of Contents

A Cold Treat Can't Be Beat

When the summer sun shines down, kids everywhere want a special treat. Not just any treat, they want ice cream!

Ice cream comes in many flavors, even some weird ones like pickle and pepper!

4

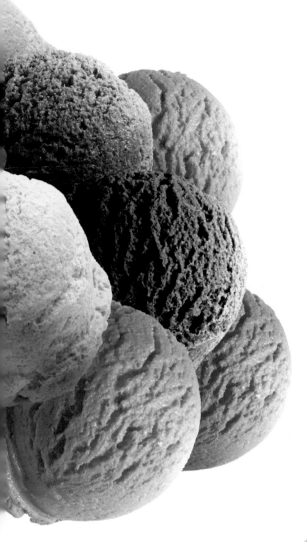

Did you know that you don't need to buy ice cream from the store? You can make this sweet treat yourself!

Ice cream is so good it has its very own day. The third Sunday in July is National Ice Cream Day in the United States.

More Than Just Ice and Cream

As much fun as it is to eat ice cream, there's a different kind of fun that comes from making your own. When you combine the **ingredients** and use some simple **science**, ice cream is the **delicious** result.

Vanilla is the world's most popular ice cream flavor.

Though some people use ice cream makers to prepare ice cream at home, most people do not have one of those machines. Do not worry, ice cream is easy to make without one.

First, gather all the ingredients

and **supplies.**

You will need:
Sugar
Whole milk
Heavy cream
Ice
Teaspoon

Salt
Gallon-sized sealable plastic bag
Quart-sized sealable plastic bag
Large bowl and measuring cups
Vanilla extract

Cool Cooking

Pour three-quarters cup (175 milliliters) of heavy cream and a quarter cup (50 milliliters) of milk into a measuring bowl.

Don't be afraid to change the recipe a bit. Add other ingredients, such as chocolate syrup or berries, to change the flavor.

Next, add three teaspoons (15 milliliters) of sugar and a half-teaspoon (2.5 milliliters) of vanilla extract.

Pour the mixture of milk, cream, sugar, and vanilla into the smaller plastic bag. Then, gently squeeze the air out of the bag and seal it.

Take the larger plastic bag and fill it about halfway with ice cubes. Crushed ice works even better.

Once there's ice in the bag, add six or eight teaspoons (30-40 milliliters) of salt to the ice. Table salt will work fine, but rock salt is better.

Salt helps **transfer** the cold from the ice to the creamy mixture inside the smaller sealed bag. This helps your mixture turn into ice cream.

Next, place the smaller sealed bag of cream, milk, sugar, and vanilla into the larger bag of ice and salt. Gently squeeze extra air from the large bag and seal it.

15

Take the large bag with the ice, salt, and smaller bag of creamy mixture inside, and shake it good and hard for 10 minutes.

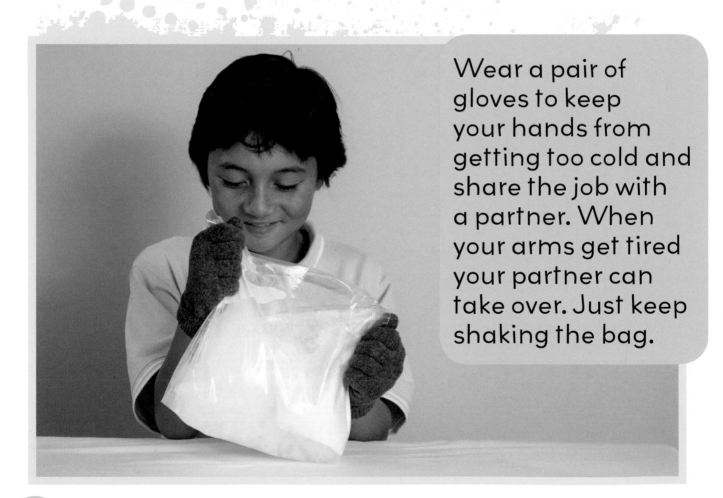

Wear a pair of gloves to keep your hands from getting too cold and share the job with a partner. When your arms get tired your partner can take over. Just keep shaking the bag.

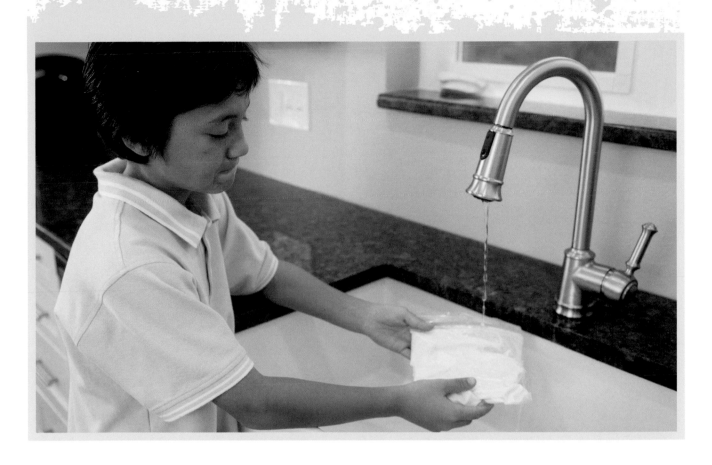

After at least 10 minutes of heavy-duty shaking, pull out the small sealed bag. Quickly rinse the salt off under cold water so none of it accidentally gets into your ice cream.

Worth the Work

After all your hard work it's time to dig in! Dish out a big scoop of ice cream and give it a taste.

In less than a half hour, you've made your tasty ice cream right at home.

Add sprinkles, chocolate sauce, or some raspberries if you like! **Toppings** add fun and flavor to your treat.

Ice cream makes people smile. It tastes good and its cold creaminess feels good on a hot day.

With a few ingredients, a little patience, and a bit of work, anyone can make their own ice cream. It really is the icy treat that can't be beat!

Photo Glossary

delicious (de-LISH-uhss): Very pleasing to taste.

ingredients (in-GREE-dee-uhntss): Separate items something is made from.

science (SYE-uhnss): The study of the physical world through experimentation.

supplies (suh-PLAHYZ): Other tools or materials needed for a recipe.

toppings (TOP-eengs): Things that can be added to food, such as chocolate sauce, nuts, or sprinkles.

transfer (TRANSS-fur): To move from one object or material to another.

Index

Websites to Visit

www.whatscookingamerica.net/desserts/
    homemadeicecream

www.sweet.seriouseats.com

www.icecream.com

Meet The Author!
www.meetREMauthors.com

About the Author

Tom Greve lives in Chicago with his wife and two children. He grew up in Wisconsin, which is America's dairy land. Since ice cream is a dairy-based treat, he has been an expert at eating it for decades.

www.rourkeeducationalmedia.com

PHOTO CREDITS: All photography by Lisa Marshall Photography except: page 5 © M. Unal Ozmen/shutterstock; page 7 Valentyn Volkov/shutterstock; page 20 © M. Unal Ozmen/shutterstock; page 22 bottom pic © CroMary/shutterstock

Edited by: Keli Sipperley

Cover design and Interior design: by Nicola Stratford
www.nicolastratford.com

Library of Congress PCN Data

How to Make Ice Cream/ Tom Greve
(Step-By-Step Projects)
ISBN 978-1-63430-353-8 (hard cover)
ISBN 978-1-63430-453-5 (soft cover)
ISBN 978-1-63430-551-8 (e-Book)
Library of Congress Control Number: 2014934348

Rourke Educational Media
Printed in the United States of America, North Mankato, Minnesota

Also Available as:
ROURKE'S e-Books